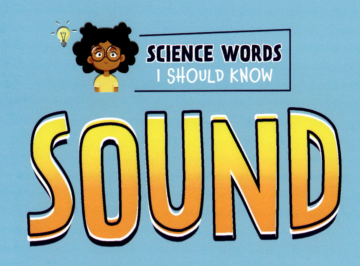

SOUND

by Julie K. Lundgren

Published in the United States of America by Cherry Lake Publishing Group
Ann Arbor, Michigan
www.cherrylakepublishing.com

Reading Adviser: Beth Walker Gambro, MS, Ed., Reading Consultant, Yorkville, IL

Photo Credits:
© Nicoleta Ionescu/Shutterstock, (cartoon girl on cover and throughout book), © VisualArtStudio/Shutterstock, (photo) cover; © Cassette Bleue/Shutterstock, speech bubbles throughout; © BongkarnGraphic/Shutterstock, (girl), © Roquillo Tebar/Shutterstock, (boy) page 5; © Pixel-Shot/Shutterstock, (boy), © Montenegro/Shutterstock, (donkey), © TashaBubo/Shutterstock, (seal), page 6; © Zivica Kerkez/Shutterstock, page 7; © BlueRingMedia/Shutterstock, page 8; © pensandoenmon/Shutterstock, page 9; © Krakenimages.com/Shutterstock, page 10; © COZ/Shutterstock, (top), © Krakenimages.com/Shutterstock, (bottom), page 11; © Lauren Suryanata/Shutterstock, (top), © luckyluke007/Shutterstock, (bottom, editorial use only) page 12; © New Africa/Shutterstock, (top), © FamVeld/Shutterstock, page 13; © Beneda Miroslav/Shutterstock, (top), © Vikulin/Shutterstock, (bottom), page 14; © Janeberry/Shutterstock, (ear), © March Studio Shutterstock, (ocean), page 15; © GraphicsRF.com/Shutterstock, page 16 and 17 (top), © LightField Studios/Shutterstock, (bottom), page 16, © Pepermpron/Shutterstock, (bottom), page 17; © Bany's beautiful art/Shutterstock, page 18 and 19 (illustrations), © Michael K. McDermott/Shutterstock, page 18 (photo), © PeopleImages.com - Yuri A /Shutterstock, (photo), page 19; © gan chaonan /Shutterstock, (photo of air and water), © Kung37 /Shutterstock, (photo of girl), page 20; © New Africa /Shutterstock, (kids), © FooTToo /Shutterstock, (fairground, editorial use only), page 21

Produced by bluedooreducation.com for Cherry Lake Publishing

Copyright © 2026 by Cherry Lake Publishing Group

All rights reserved. No part of this book may be reproduced or utilized in any form or by any means without written permission from the publisher.

Library of Congress Cataloging-in-Publication Data has been filed and is available at catalog.loc.gov.

Printed in the United States of America

Note from Publisher: Websites change regularly, and their future contents are outside of our control. Supervise children when conducting any recommended online searches for extended learning opportunities.

TABLE OF CONTENTS

Sound All Around............................ 4

Sound Is Energy.............................. 8

Good Vibes 10

Hear Here 15

Think About It.................................22
Glossary 23
Find Out More.................................24
Index 24
About the Author............................24

SOUND ALL AROUND

Look at the cover of this book.
What is the boy doing?

People get information about the world around them through sound.

Headphones, speakers, and bullhorns all help carry sound.

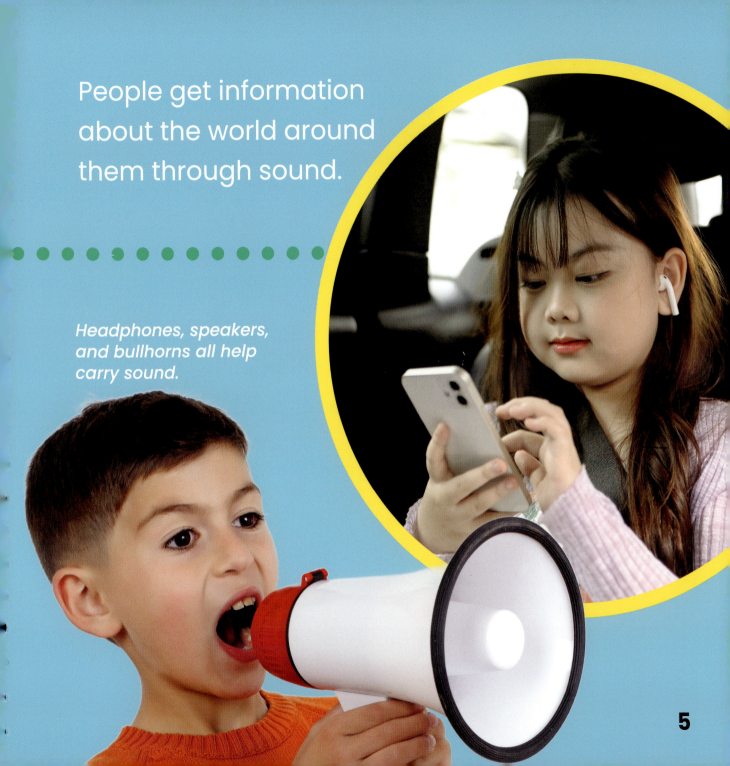

5

People and most animals use ears to hear sound.

Ears come in many shapes and sizes.

With sound, we can listen for danger and **communicate**.

SOUND IS ENERGY

Energy is the power that makes something work, move, or change.

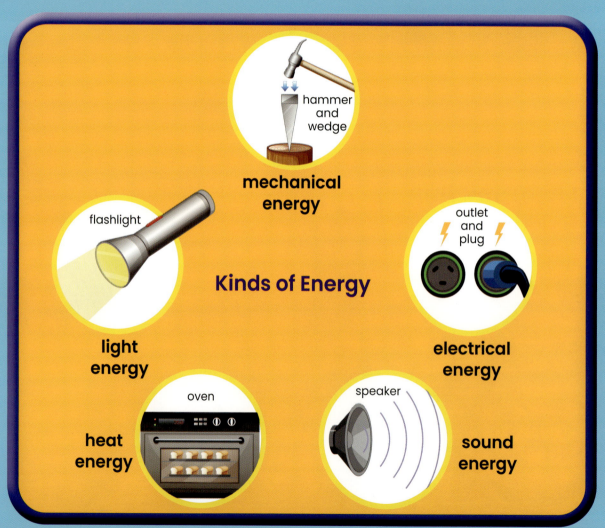

Energy stored in the batteries will make the toy car move.

There are different kinds of energy. Sound is one kind of energy.

GOOD VIBES

Things make sound when they vibrate. The **vibrations** are sound energy.

Vibrate means to move back and forth very fast.

When you pluck a guitar string, you can hear and see it vibrate.

Vibrations make cymbals crash and hollow drums thump and pop.

Say Ahhhhhhh!
Place your fingers gently on your throat. Hum or say something. Can you feel vibrations?

11

The speed of vibrations is a sound's **pitch**.

A sound has low pitch when its **source** vibrates slowly.

Our ears hear deep sounds like big engines and bullfrogs.

A sound has high pitch when its source vibrates quickly.

The sharp screech of a whistle or baby says "Attention, now!"

13

Size can affect pitch. The big tuba has a lower pitch than the smaller trumpet.

trumpet

tuba

HEAR HERE

Sound vibrations travel in waves.

Like waves on the sea, sound waves have peaks and valleys.

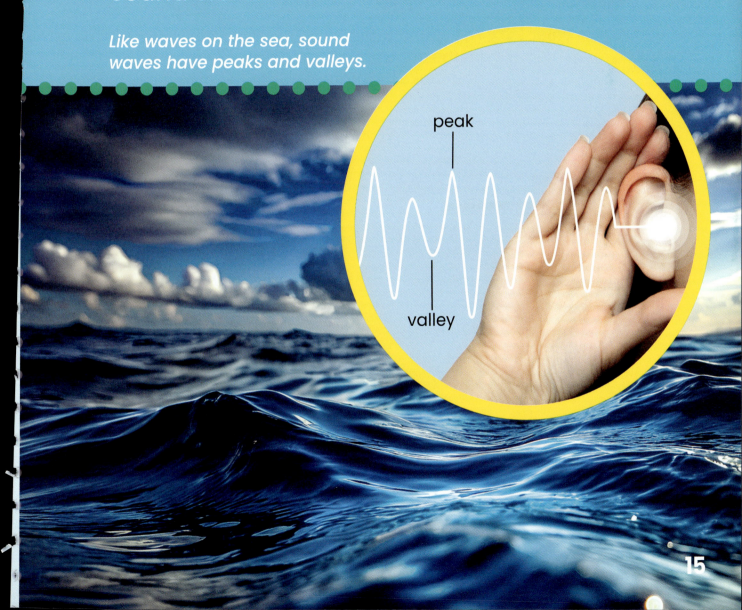

How do human ears use sound waves to hear?

1 Sound waves enter your ear.

2 The sound waves hit the eardrum and make it vibrate.

3 The vibrations are sent as messages to the brain.

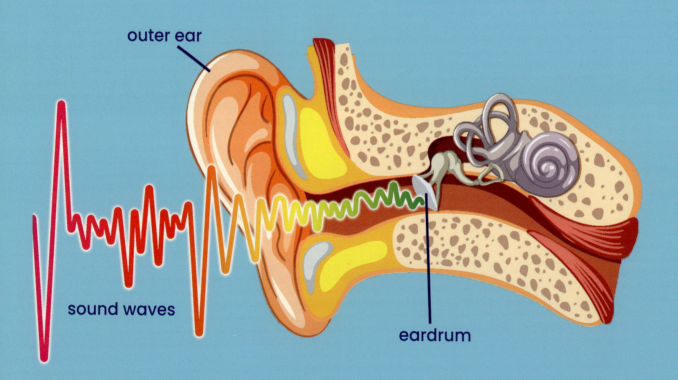

outer ear

sound waves

eardrum

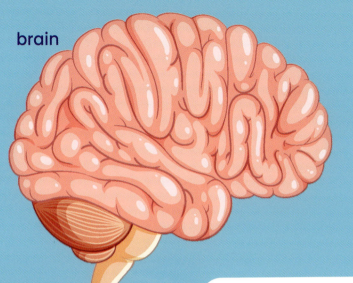

brain

Your brain uses the messages to tell you what sounds you are hearing.

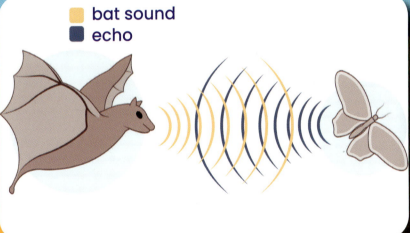

bat sound
echo

Bouncing Sound
Bats make sounds and use the **echoes** to find their way and hunt for food. This is called echolocation.

echolocation:
EH-koh-loh-KAY-shuhn

Sound wave **frequency** makes sounds loud or soft. Sound is LOUD when the distance between peaks is short.

Sound is soft when the distance between peaks is long.

Low Frequency

It takes time for sound waves to travel to our ears. They move slowest through gases, like air.

Sound waves move faster through water than through air.

20

THINK ABOUT IT

Using what you have learned in this book, match each sentence to the correct picture.

1 This shows low frequency.

2 This large animal makes a loud sound.

3 This animal uses echoes to hunt.

4 This shows high frequency.

A.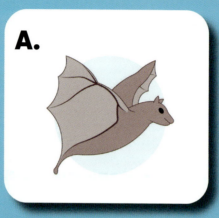

B.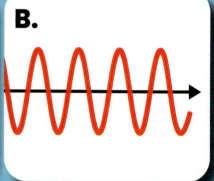

C.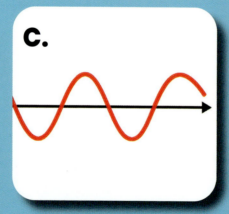

D.

Answers: 1C 2D 3A 4B

22

GLOSSARY

communicate (kuh-MYOO-nuh-kayt) share messages or information through sound or actions

echoes (EH-kohz) the reflection of sound waves off an object

frequency (FREE-kwen-see) how often something happens in a set amount of time

pitch (PICH) describes the highness or lowness of a sound

solids (SAH-lidz) objects that hold their shape

source (SORS) the place where something begins or comes from

vibrations (vie-BRAY-shuhnz) fast back and forth movements

Find Out More

Books
Bernhardt, Caroline. *Science Starters: Sound,* Minnetonka, MN: Bellwether Media, 2018

Rake, Jody Sullivan. *What Is Sound?* Mankato, MN: Pebble Books, 2019

Websites
Search these online sources with an adult:

Sound | Kiddle

Sound | Science Trek

Index

air 20
ears 6, 16, 20
energy 8, 9
echolocation 17
frequency 18, 19
pitch 12, 13, 14
speed 12
vibrate(s) 10, 12, 13, 16
wave(s) 15, 16, 18, 20, 21

About the Author

Julie K. Lundgren grew up in northern Minnesota near Lake Superior. She delighted in picking berries, finding cool rocks, and trekking in the woods. She still does! Julie's interest in nature science led her to a degree in biology. She adores her family, her sweet cat, and Adventure Days.